The Little Red Sports Car

A Modern Fable About Diabetes

Written By Eleanor Troutt • Illustrated By J. Chris Price

©2007 by Eleanor Troutt
All rights reserved

Written by Eleanor Troutt
Illustrated by J Chris Price

ISBN 0-615-13281-2

Once upon a time, not too long ago, there was a little red sports car. His name was Rudy and he lived in a pleasant town with a nice owner who took very good care of him.

There were lots of good roads and first-rate garages in the town and Rudy was very happy.

*H*is owner, whose name was Bob, took Rudy in for regular check-ups and fed him only the best fuel and motor oil.

And Rudy, in return, tried to give Bob the very best service he could.

But one day, Bob noticed a strange noise coming from Rudy's engine whenever he changed from one gear to another.

Puzzled and worried, Bob took Rudy into a garage and asked for their best mechanic to try to find out what was wrong.

Bob hovered around, worried and anxious in case anything serious might be wrong.

*F*inally, after what seemed to be a long time,
the mechanic turned to Bob and said,
"I'm sorry but I'm afraid I have some bad news for you."
"Oh no! What's wrong?!" Bob exclaimed.

"Well," explained the mechanic,
"Your little car has developed a unique problem
which happens once in awhile -
even to the healthiest of cars."

Now Bob was really concerned. "How serious is this?!" he said in alarm. "Will we still be able to drive around together?"

However, he didn't get to worry about that for long because the mechanic continued, "You'll also have to put a special additive in the motor oil from now on. This is easy to get but you'll have to be careful not to add too much or too little or Rudy could land back in the garage pretty fast!"

Bob still had a lot of questions so he readily agreed to meet with the specialist and an appointment was set up that very day before Rudy was even permitted to leave the garage.

Bob learned to put in just the right amount of the special motor additive and he learned to pay close attention to the new dials and gauges, which the specialist had suggested he install.

*R*udy was very anxious to please, so he tried his best to make it as easy on Bob as he could. And he certainly felt better once the special additive was added to his oil!

I'm happy to say that this story has a happy ending. On any sunny day, you can see Rudy and Bob touring around the countryside just as happy as they can be!

And you'd never know what a life-changing experience they had been through unless you asked!